The Little Book About Purpose
That Everyone Should Read

Yolanda G. Stewart

Copyright © 2023 Yolanda G. Stewart

All rights reserved. This book or any portion thereof may not be reproduced or used in any manner whatsoever without the express written permission of the publisher, except for the use of brief quotations in a book review.

Scripture quotations marked KJV are from the King James Version of the Holy Bible.

Scripture quotations marked NLT are taken from the *Holy Bible*, New Living Translation, copyright © 1996, 2004, 2015 by Tyndale House Foundation. Used by permission of Tyndale House Publishers, Inc., Carol Stream, Illinois 60188. All rights reserved.

Scripture quotations taken from the Amplified® Bible (AMP), Copyright © 2015 by The Lockman Foundation. Used by permission. lockman.org

Scripture quotations marked (ESV) are from The ESV® Bible (The Holy Bible, English Standard Version®), copyright © 2001 by Crossway, a publishing ministry of Good News Publishers. Used by permission. All rights reserved.

Scripture quotations marked NKJV are taken from the New King James Version®. Copyright © 1982 by Thomas Nelson. Used by permission. All rights reserved.

Scripture quotations marked NIV are taken from The Holy Bible, New International Version® NIV® Copyright © 1973, 1978, 1984, 2011 by Biblica, Inc. Used with permission. All rights reserved worldwide.

Printed in the United States of America

First Printing, 2023

ISBN: 8988256502

ISBN-13: 979-8-9882565-0-2

My Deepest Gratitude

To my husband, Damon. Thank you for your love, support and always being my biggest cheerleader. Thank you for being a patient listener and for all of the sacrifices you made to support my assignment to write this book. You make it easy to live on purpose. I love you honey.

To the memory of my dear mom. I am thankful for her love and encouragement. I can hear her voice echoing how proud she is of me.

To my amazing children, Damon II, Jasmin, Donovan, and my bonus daughter and son, Linmary and Kevin. May this book answer your questions and equip you to live yielded to God's purpose.

To my awesome grandchildren, Ayden, Janiyah, Alijah, Avery and Axel-Damon- May you live in full surrender to his purpose.

Your nana loves you!

Table of Contents

Foreword by Anthony D. Daley Sr. v

Foreword by James Stockdale vi

Foreword by Marcus Tankard vii

Foreword by Jennifer Johnson viii

Acknowledgments ix

Introduction 1

Principle #1: Purpose Is Not What You Spend Your Life Searching For, But What You Spend Your Life Yielding To 3

    The Power of Surrender 8

    The Beauty of Harmony 16

    The Danger of Discord 22

Principle #2: Purpose Is the Master, and Zeal Is the Servant 29

    Enemies of Purpose 35

    The Subtlety of Disobedience 42

    Comfortable Resistance 48

    Generational Impact 52

Principle #3: Purpose Serves the King's Pleasure 59

    Kingdom-centered Prayer 65

    Get in Step 72

    Repentance Is a Kingdom Strategy 76

Principle #4: Purpose Is Eternal 81

    Redeem the Time 81

    Perpetual Grace 87

    Every Season Is Your Season 92

About the Author 99

Foreword by Anthony D. Daley Sr.

Credibility is not gained based on knowledge, but experience is the best qualifier. I have served alongside Yolanda Stewart for many years and have a front-row seat to witness what it looks like for someone to live on purpose. She is a person who values purpose over position and will always sacrifice the temporary for the eternal.

This book will bring a person into the right perspective and empower a life of purpose by pushing back on the modern-day colloquialisms that sound correct but are a mental trap that will rob us from living on purpose.

Yolanda takes the guesswork from the wrestling match of life's questions: "Why am I here?" "What is my purpose?" She does this by pointing us back to the strategic partnership with our Creator, who fashioned us uniquely and uses all our life experiences as a point of conveyance to fulfill a purpose broader than ourselves. She simplifies what has been viewed as a complicated equation of discovery by raising the value of yielding and responding to the Holy Spirit's daily promptings.

I love how Yolanda offers applications to the information shared in these pages. She understands that information without application does not lead to life change. In keeping with her leadership values, she delivers practicalities that are easily applied. She offers sound examples and clear action steps that help us embrace the promptings with the correct responses.

If you want a life that is both fulfilling and impactful, find a quiet place, open the pages of this book, and carefully and intentionally digest the content of each page. When you reach the end, close the book and start practicing the principles. The result will be a life that makes a difference now and continues to empower long after you have completed your journey.

—Anthony D. Daley Sr., Pastor, Mosaic Church, Clarksville, TN

Foreword by James Stockdale

It was only the second time my wife, Pam, and I had attended the Tabernacle Church. We glanced a knowing look at each other as a graceful, articulate woman took the microphone and began to speak. She had taken command of the room and our attention just by her presence. She postured herself as a leader and spoke with vision and voice that confirmed as much. Here was a woman who understood her purpose.

We leaned into the moment as she spoke. That was our first exposure to Yolanda Stewart. That was November of 2014, and we knew our paths would cross again. A short time later, through a set of unusual circumstances, I joined the staff of that church and had the privilege of working alongside her for eighteen months.

During that time, I learned to listen when Lieutenant Colonel Yolanda Stewart spoke. Not because I had to, but because I wanted to.

The book you hold in your hand contains vital information you need. My advice is simple: if you have not bought it, buy it. If you have bought it, read it. You will discover, as we did that day in 2014, Yolanda has more than information about purpose, she understands the subject and expresses it eloquently.

The concepts and ideas found in this book are well-crafted and scripturally sound. Yolanda's thoughtful insight will gently nudge you to unlearn some things, while enlightening you on others. She will answer questions you have thought about but were afraid to ask for fear of being misunderstood.

This book is a must-read for anyone seeking to understand their purpose in life or for anyone seeking a deeper understanding about why they were born. You will be surprised just how easy it is to live on purpose.

—James Stockdale, President, Latin American Ministry

Foreword by Marcus Tankard

I want you to prepare your heart for the journey you are about to embark on. As you travel the pages of this masterpiece, open your heart to hear what the Spirit is saying to you. Yolanda G. Stewart has her ear set to the mouth of the Father. The precision, tact, understanding, and sheer elegance by which she crafts the thoughts of God concerning His plan for your life is nothing short of a masterpiece.

Most of us have asked God the question, "Lord, why am I here?" This wonderful work of art is a guide into the Father's heart, where layer by layer He can unveil His original intention for your life.

This book is a prophetic work, and it is to be valued and prized above rubies. Paul prayed that he would have utterance to declare the mystery of the gospel. The utterance conveyed here will outline your purpose, beginning with salvation and ending in the liberating reality that God has a plan specifically for you and that is in partnership with His plan for the reconciliation of the world.

If you are serious about fulfilling God's plan for your life, I would add this book to your yearly "must-reads" list. The truths shared in this book are designed to keep you sharp and on the right path for purpose. I am honored to give you an exhortation to embrace the revelation found in the pages of this book. As you read, watch God do a new thing in you and through you.

—Marcus Tankard,

star of the hit Bravo TV reality series *Thicker Than Water*, and a missionary, pastor, musician, and author

Foreword by Jennifer Johnson

This book is speaking the inner thoughts of an entire generation. Multitudes of age brackets have passed on the notion that purpose is a destination, some grand achievement, or one singular decision. Men and women have worn themselves thin and fallen headlong into disappointment trying to insert themselves into purpose and striving to prove something to their own hearts and to God.

I believe the weeds of confusion get sown subtly because of our freedoms and comforts. We can achieve so much because of our natural freedoms. Many well-meaning people have caught and taught the language of *"doing something for God."* Whether it comes from a lack of understanding or out of their own misplaced convictions, they teach that *you are the center of achieving your purpose.* The pressure is on for you to *figure it out* so that you can fulfill it.

This book is fresh language, a clarion call, a message written plainly, a new blueprint for building a life in Christ. Yolanda's statement struck me in such a beautiful way: *"Freedom is not independence but bondage to Christ, and bondage to Christ is intentionally yielding our will to the one who crafted our purpose and holds his future."*

Yolanda also writes, *"I have reached a resolve that I will allow neither unanswered questions nor the uncertainty of the unknown to breed distrust in my heart regarding God's character."* This is just one of so many powerful statements that, if you chew on them, will nourish you to a proper perspective of purpose.

I truly believe God will use this book as a seed in the earth to shift hearts and minds into a true awakening.

—Jennifer Johnson, forever sister and friend

Acknowledgments

I am thankful for the direct and indirect insights and contributions that a variety of people have made to this book. It is indeed an amalgamation of years of study, observation, and applying the lessons learned.

I am thankful for Pastor Anthony Daley and Pastor Jim and Pam Stockdale for providing platforms of opportunities to present on this topic. I am also thankful for my friends Pastor Cheryl Smith and Regina Hoosier whose love for me sustained them as editors through the first of many rough drafts.

Thank you, Dr. Jackie Knight, for literally being the friend and resource I needed and for coming to my rescue when I was going in circles about completing this project.

To the ladies of Women Warriors connect group, thank you for every opportunity to share the messages I have received and for sharing yours. We are blessed to have each other.

Introduction

Just as [in His love] He chose us in Christ [actually selected us for Himself as His own] before the foundation of the world, so that we would be holy [that is, consecrated, set apart for Him, purpose-driven] and blameless in His sight. —**Ephesians 1:4 AMP**

If you are searching for answers to help piece together the portrait of your purpose, you have picked up the right book. The Bible provides the clearest blueprint of purpose, and my endeavor is to help you connect the dots through scriptures, practical illustrations, and personal stories.

I want to be honest with you. I must have quit and given up writing this book one hundred times. I must have rewritten the pages twice as many times as I quit. The Lord would not let me let it go. Lord knows, I wanted to.

To accomplish this work of love, it has taken many hours for me to push beyond my internal obstacles, all while life was happening around me.

Here we are. Here it is. The book that I was chosen to write. I am thrilled to share what I have learned thus far because there is a purposeful peace waiting for you that I simply do not have words to articulate. I am in awe of God, and I know he will fulfill your earnest desire to know what it means to truly live in his purpose for your life.

Let's start at the beginning.

Our purpose was assigned to us while we were in eternity. Long before we were introduced to the world and born to our parents in time God considered his intentions, and then chose us, to fulfill them. *(Read that again.)*

Therefore, the clarity and affirmation you desperately seek can only be found in God, and he wants to reveal it by his Spirit.

He wants to relieve you of the pressure of trying to *figure it out* and replace the pressure with peace and freedom instead. These are rewards of total surrender.

Surrender positions you right in the middle of the will of the one who authored your purpose.

There is no need for you to wonder and wander through the wilderness of life, hoping to one day reach the promised land of purpose. No, those days are about to be over for you. You are about to enter a new level of certainty and freedom.

Get ready.

By the time you finish reading this book, it is my prayer that you will be convinced that no matter where you find yourself, you will be certain of the perpetual workings of purpose in you and through you.

In fact, the closer you draw to God, the closer he will draw to you and reveal more of himself, as you discover more about yourself, in him. This is what purposeful living looks like.

God never promised the creature all the answers to life's perplexing questions. However, we can be encouraged that he wants to teach us that certainty is possible, even with unanswered questions and missing details that we may never know. He has set it up so that faith in God is required for us to be led by God. Furthermore, since our purpose originated in the mind of God, how can we ever expect to fulfill it independent of a relationship with him.

In these pages, I hope to offer the clarity that you need. It may require you to unlearn what we all have been taught in exchange for **_learning to know God's will_**, God's way (see Romans 12:2).

I am offering four principles to help you begin learning to know God's will for your life. As you embrace them, you will become an open door for the Holy Spirit to customize the message.

So, let's dive in and begin the conversation.

Principle #1

Purpose Is Not What You Spend Your Life Searching For, But What You Spend Your Life Yielding To

Don't copy the behavior and customs of this world, but let God transform you into a new person by changing the way you think. Then you will learn to know God's will for you, which is good and pleasing and perfect. —**Romans 12:2 NLT**

This principle has marked me for life. It has set me free from the burden of a perceived responsibility to figure it out on my own. God never intended for me to figure out his intentions for me. It has always been his will to reveal them through the process of yielding. *Read that again.*

Now I can breathe and live in the confidence that comes from knowing that my relationship with the Lord Jesus is the access point to purpose-filled living. When I yield, I have assurance that his purpose is being fulfilled in me and through me. *(Whew! It is just that simple.)*

I am beginning to learn the workings of purpose and my soul is confident and at peace.

This same confidence has become a powerful influence in every area of my life. Now I live with a determination to be obedient and alert for however the Spirit wants to partner with me. I am finally living for his purpose.

For so long, I had complicated the entire process. I thought the purpose for my life was to accomplish *one big thing* that God had hidden somewhere in my future.

I thought my responsibility was to figure it out before I was too old to enjoy it, not realizing that His purposes were already working when I surrendered my life to him.

I thought that everything leading up to the *discovery of my purpose* was insignificant. I thought God's plans wouldn't begin until I had made the *discovery* or accomplished the *one big thing* and then at that point, I would be *living my purpose.*

Modern culture has offered strategies and pathways that are a complete contradiction to the roadmap we see in scriptures. For too long, we have believed what modern culture has taught us about purpose.

We were taught that purpose is the life project or good deed that wakes you up at night or gets you out of bed in the morning. We were taught that purpose is the area where you are most gifted; or the one skill that you have mastered.

News Flash!

They are wrong!

Purpose exceeds the scope of projects, passion, gifts, and talents. It involves the tangible and intangible. It is a collaborative combination of people, experiences, timelines, thought processes and so many other intricate details. It is too much to fully comprehend.

One common misconception is confusing platforms and opportunities for life purpose when they are simply pieces of a much bigger picture.

God will use roles, responsibilities, job titles, or special skills as platforms. God will use them to process, prepare, and posture us to accomplish his intentions but they should not be mistaken for *purpose itself.*

If I could shout it from a mountain top, I would. Modern culture taught us wrong! They taught us many lessons about purpose that we must unlearn. If you have gotten this far in the book, the unlearning has already begun.

Now that I know what I know, I refuse to allow my life to be a cheap *substitute*.

The passage in Romans is foundational. Paul begins with important instructions for living and *learning to know God's will* for us. He warns us not to copy the customs of *modern culture*, with their counter-kingdom ideologies.

Instead, he has proposed surrender as the starting point for the transformation and understanding we so desperately need. We need to think differently, to discern what he wants to show us about his will for us. He is the only one we can trust to reveal his intentions.

We must reach a resolve that we will allow neither unanswered questions nor the uncertainty of the unknown to breed distrust in our heart regarding God's character.

Instead, we must trust him to lead us to the fulfillment of his intentions in us and through us.

Our greatest responsibility is to live yielded and be led by his Spirit. When we do, we will be able to see his workings in the good, the bad and the ugly situations of our lives.

I know this may be the first time you have heard it like this, but that is what sets this book apart from any other book you may have read. It is God's prerogative to leverage anything about our life to accomplish his intentions. That includes our strengths and weaknesses, gifts and talents, preferences and even pain.

Your Thoughts on a Lifetime of Yielding to Purpose

Purpose is not what you spend your life searching for, but purpose is what you spend your life yielding to.

The Power of Surrender

Therefore, I urge you, brothers and sisters, by the mercies of God, to present your bodies [dedicating all of yourselves, set apart] as a living sacrifice, holy and well-pleasing to God, which is your rational (logical, intelligent) act of worship. And do not be conformed to this world [any longer with its superficial values and customs], but be transformed and progressively changed [as you mature spiritually] by the renewing of your mind [focusing on godly values and ethical attitudes], so that you may prove [for yourselves] what the will of God is, that which is good and acceptable and perfect [in His plan and purpose for you]. **—Romans 12:1-2 AMP**

A lifestyle of yielding to God *(presenting yourself)* will result in a lifestyle of transformation where we get the word *metamorphosis*. This word in the Greek combines two words *meta* and *morphoo*. In short, it means to experience change in how you think, feel and behave as a result of consistently being with someone.

Essentially, you *surrender* your identity and ideology in exchange for his.

I believe that the process of transformation is what God uses to restore us to the *default settings (his original intent)* when he chose us in him. Imagine how it would please God if when thinking of purpose, rather than overriding the intention of our creator, we *defaulted to surrender*.

It is time to raise the white flag. Raising a white flag has been the universal symbol of surrender for centuries. It conveys one has intentionally relinquished their will and power to another.

Surrender is total submission and vulnerability. *(Are you seeing the portrait I am painting?)*

I am aiming to make the point that divine *defaults* are the values God assigned at the place of origination *(Remember, we were in him before we were in the world)*. Restoration to the defaults happens when we surrender to the required changes to our way of thinking, believing and behaving. In doing so, we become more efficient and effective in the accomplishment of the _Creator's original intentions_.

He has given us the power of the Holy Spirit who works in us, giving us the desire and the power to do what pleases him. This is our ultimate _default setting_.

> _Yet God has made everything beautiful for its own time. He has planted eternity in the human heart, but even so, people cannot see the whole scope of God's work from beginning to end._
> **—Ecclesiastes 3:11 NLT**

Deep inside we have a knowing that there is more to life than what we see and can figure out. Even the heavens and the earth declare and reveal God to us.

I love using practical analogies to help me explain spiritual principles. _(Just stick with me until I can make it plain.)_

Knowing God has placed eternity in my heart sparks my curiosity. I'm asking, "Lord, tell me more. Help me understand what this means and what is it supposed to produce?"

Here is what came to mind when reading the phrase "He has planted eternity in the human heart": An internal, _"eternity receiver"_ that allows our spirit to receive signals _in time_, from the _realm of eternity_. It works like an internal knowing and awareness, that God uses to give us hope beyond our present, physical existence. This hope in him compels us to a different standard of living. We choose to accept or ignore it.

The reception of the receiver works best when our heart is yielded.

Without _yielding to the point of surrender and transformation,_ we will never fulfill his original intentions for our lives.

There is much to learn and understand and it begins with yielding to the point that something supernatural happens to our will and perspective.

May we raise the white flag of surrender and give ourselves fully, to God's good pleasure.

One way to know that you are operating in the default setting of surrender is when your deepest desire is to fulfill his will over your own. Functioning at this level of surrender, everything becomes meaningless in comparison to pleasing the Lord.

Are you willing to reconsider every plan that you were once determined to execute? Are you willing to abandon the best job you ever had at the prompting of his Spirit? Are you willing to forfeit the scholarship that you worked so hard to earn? Are you willing to break off the engagement with the one you were certain was sent by God?

If you can answer yes to these questions, celebrate the progress, and don't look back. This is an indication that you have partnered with the Lord's intention to reset you to the defaults.

At the default settings we are no longer seeking a substitute sacrifice in place of obedience and surrender. Because now we understand that we (through obedience and surrender) are the only sacrifice he desires.

In a later chapter I will talk more about Saul and his choice to offer God a sacrifice as a substitute for obedience. Saul's delusion was thinking that it was an acceptable alternative. Paul says the only acceptable sacrifice to God is one that is living and intentionally surrendered.

God is intentional with his language in the Scriptures when he requires us to <u>willingly die to ourselves</u>, so we can be <u>a living sacrifice</u> to redeem those whom he loves. *This makes yielding worth it all.*

I avoid Facebook, but on occasion I come across nuggets of gold, and this is one of them: "Living for God requires a toe tag."

Sometimes obedience and surrender are easier said than done. So, I want to continue the conversation about surrender with a personal story, because its power cannot be overstated.

I want to do my best to ensure that what I am challenging you to do is relatable, realistic, and attainable. If that requires me to be uncomfortably transparent, oh well. Here we go.

When I began dating my husband, we were just fifteen years young. I had yielded my life to Jesus just two years prior. I was young and excited about being *saved*. I was telling anyone who would listen. The icing on the cake was that I had found true love, and his name was Damon Anthony Stewart.

Can you imagine the struggle in our flesh? Don't make me spell it out. Let's just say, in those days I did a lot of repenting for the same sin.

Here is a powerful point about surrender when you find yourself in a trap set by the enemy: although I was in a sin trap, I didn't change my mind about the sin of fornication. *(Read that again.)*

I knew it was wrong, but I didn't justify my sin nor make excuses. Instead, I agreed with God and pleaded for help. He helped me and restored me to a place of strength so that I could reset my flesh to be in line with his truth.

What I knew and believed about sin was my way of escape. It is what the Lord used to rescue me from myself. I held on to the truth about sin, even when my actions were inconsistent. *"You shall know the truth, and the truth shall make you free"* (John 8:32 NKJV).

I want you to understand this principle: the value I placed on truth set me free from the slavery of the sin trap. When we surrender to truth it will always produce freedom.

My willingness to agree with what the truth says about sin was the open door that eventually provoked repentance and surrender once and for all. From the point of restoration, we were set free from the trap of fornication and were empowered to abstain until marriage.

I want to be clear: the Lord didn't remove the struggle, but he ministered strength to endure without compromise.

This takes me to the account of Jesus praying at the Mount of Olives, leading up to his crucifixion. There is a connection that I want you to see.

Luke gives the details concerning when Jesus prayed: *"Father, if you are willing, please take this cup of suffering away from me. Yet I want your will to be done, not mine.' Then an angel from heaven appeared and strengthened him"* (Luke 22:42-43 NLT).

He prayed to the Father to take the cup away and in this account, Jesus' preference was actively contending with God's purpose, but his caveat is king. *"Yet I want your will to be done, not mine."*

Jesus was modeling a prayer principle under pressure. When Jesus surrendered to purpose, he was strengthened. He still had to walk through the struggle, but he was strengthened to endure.

I want you to see that surrender positions you to be strengthened, because it conveys the exchange of independence for dependency.

Freedom is not independence but bondage to Christ, and bondage to Christ is intentionally yielding our will to the one who crafted our purpose and holds our future.

So when *(not if, but when)* you find yourself struggling to surrender your passions and preferences, struggle if you must but don't dismiss the necessity of surrender.

The more you draw to the Lord the less you will struggle with surrender, though you will never be completely free from the struggle of surrender until your final transformation to your heavenly body *(smile)*.

Because we are human, we can expect to have struggles on the journey. Here is a piece of advice for the road:

When preferences and passion are contending with your ability to yield to purpose, remember that they make terrible tour guides. Your life will be better off being led by his Spirit.

Your Thoughts on "The Power of Surrender"

Surrender positions you to be strengthened because it is the exchange of independence for dependency.

The Beauty of Harmony

If possible, so far as it depends on you, live peaceably with all.
—**Romans 12:18 ESV**

Figuratively speaking, God never intended us to be a solo act, write the script, or star in our own production.

On the contrary, our life is intended to be lived under the *direction* of *the Holy Spirit, the conductor,* and in harmony with those that we encounter on the journey. God uses relationships to accomplish His purpose. In the context of this metaphor of purpose, the Conductor leads the orchestra of varied instruments *(people),* each making their *unique sounds (purpose-filled words and actions).* Although separate and distinct, when they follow the conductor, each sound compliments one another and produces a sound that pleases God.

Understanding this principle is crucial to how we see and navigate relationships.

*So then, let us aim for harmony in the church
and try to build each other up.* —**Romans 14:19 NLT**

Some encounters are strictly platonic, and *notes (purpose-filled words or actions)* are never exchanged. We are just passing by. I see you and you see me, but that is the extent of it. These are the people you pass on Interstate 40E that you will never see again *(maybe).*

What about the relationships that are painful, woeful, and counterproductive to who we are becoming? God has a plan for them, too. We must find peace in knowing that God intends to use even these relationships to cultivate our character and perpetuate His kingdom-centered plans. I do not claim to know how; I just know that he can and will.

When a relationship becomes difficult, my prayer is "Lord, what is my responsibility in this relationship? Help me render the response that partners with your intentions. And Lord, protect my soul; do not let this destroy me. Help me not to mess it up by getting caught up in the web of strife, unforgiveness, bitterness, fear etc. Help me. Amen." *(I needed this prayer, like right now!)*

Then there are relationships that are mutually beneficial, in which harmony is almost immediate.

May God, who gives this patience and encouragement, help you live in complete harmony with each other, as is fitting for followers of Christ Jesus. —**Romans 15:5 NLT**

Patience and encouragement are needed if we are going to live in harmony. Living in harmony with others is what Christ-followers do. *(Let us read it again together.)*

This scripture and metaphor really resonate with me because I am a musician. My voice is my instrument, so I am getting this deep down into my soul and spirit.

Regardless of the relationship, it is important that we keep our eyes on the Conductor so we will know which *note (purpose-filled words or actions)* to play. We must care enough about people to seek harmony because, among many other things, offense disrupts harmony. Offense distorts the notes of others because it is filtered through personal filters rather than the Conductor himself. Confusion and pride are the things the Conductor warns us about.

Since we are living by the Spirit, let us follow the Spirit's leading in every part of our lives. —**Galatians 5:25 NLT**

Another translation articulates the message even clearer: *"If we live by the Spirit, let us also keep in step with the Spirit"* (Galatians 5:25 ESV).

Paul was an instrument of purpose when he penned the letters of the New Testament under the inspiration of the Holy Spirit. Reading his writings, we hear the sound he left on the earth. Our agreement with what the Holy Spirit said through Paul gives him influence in our life and creates harmony that pleases God. *(Did you catch it?)*

Since I am not smart enough to know God's plan for your life, my chief role in your life is to live in intimate proximity to the Conductor so that I can discern which *note (purpose-filled words or actions)* I need to play to be in harmony with his intentions for our relationship.

We should live with the expectation that he will put us in relationship with those we were created to harmonize with. If we follow his lead, we will be in rhythm and harmony.

Now that I have a better understanding of the potential deeper purpose of every relationship, I am more intentional to seek the leadership of the Holy Spirit concerning each one. Knowing what we just learned, relationships must never again be business as usual.

I believe God's intention is to use us all as instruments of purpose to produce *a sound (purpose-filled words or actions)* to showcase his love and power. He has invited us all to a partnership of reconciliation.

According to Paul's teachings in 2 Corinthians 5, we have been given the ministry of reconciliation. As ministers of reconciliation, we plead with and point people to Jesus through our prayers and encouraging messages, and through living by example.

I want to use the accounting definition of reconciliation to help you understand the spiritual meaning. In my example, people represent *the accounts,* and the word of God represents *the statements.*

Routine reconciliation is the best *practice* of any successful accountant. During this process, the accountant verifies, analyzes, and compares the numbers to ensure the accounts agree with the statements. When a discrepancy is identified, the accountant works until the discrepancy is resolved.

Like an accountant, a successful Christ-follower must yield to the process of reconciliation in their own life, while partnering with God in the same process in others.

In doing so, we must routinely verify, analyze, and compare our lives with the principles of righteous living to ensure we're living in agreement, and make time to address the discrepancies.

When we pray for someone to receive healing, we are essentially praying that their body *(the account)* comes into agreement with the word of God *(the statement)* that says by his stripes we are healed (Isaiah 53:5).

When we pray for the salvation of friends, we pray that they will repent and surrender to the work of the Holy Spirit. This is the process necessary for them to live *(the account)* according to his intentions *(the statement)* from the foundation of the world.

This is what purposeful living looks like.

As harmony becomes a lifestyle, when we miss our cues, lose the rhythm, release the wrong sound, or forget our part, it will stand out.

The gospel of Jesus Christ is all about reconciliation. Repentance is all about the work of reconciliation. Prayers are all about reconciliation.

Your Thoughts on "The Beauty of Harmony"

*As harmony becomes a
lifestyle, when we miss our
cues, lose the rhythm,
release the wrong sound,
or forget our part,
it will stand out.*

The Danger of Discord

Discord *(disagreement with God and conflict with others)* is a fact of life. I am under no delusion. It is not always easy to practice Christ-like qualities toward others, especially difficult people. The struggle to harmonize is real. But it is easier when I remember how God loved me and chose me even in the condition he found me.

What I am certain of is that we can mature in our perspective of our relationship with God and with others to the point that living in discord is woefully uncomfortable. So much so that even the thought of discord provokes and compels us to reconcile back to harmony *(agreement with God)*.

Recently this thought occurred to me: sometimes we equate chronological experience with spiritual maturity. We expect people who have been following Christ for a long time to demonstrate a high degree of spiritual maturity.

We are wrong!

In my experience with *church people*, sometimes it has been the ones who have been in church for years that are spiritually immature, stirring discord.

The obvious discord is easy to identify. For instance, living in contention and disagreement with the Word of God and practicing disobedience. However, we may need some help pointing out the subtler characteristics. *(I am here to help.)*

Take, for instance, secret strife, gossip, and unforgiveness. What about the sometimes-subtle discord of self-righteousness, pride, jealousy, and selfishness? Since we are on a roll, we can also toss in the discord of excuses, poor prioritization, and procrastination with kingdom assignments. *(I slipped in a few that you likely were not expecting.)*

Discord has its own, boastful voice, justifying its sound and influence in our lives. It can be aggressive and consume us. Discord can cause relationships to spiral out of control to the point where you blatantly disregard what the Conductor is saying. Intense conflict and strife can result in the voice of the Conductor falling on deaf ears.

I must admit, I am all too familiar with the pangs of longing to hear the same voice of the Conductor for directions after I have repeatedly refused to follow his lead for correction.

God has given us power by his Spirit, so we are without excuse when we find ourselves living in discord.

> *The temptations in your life are no different from what others experience. And God is faithful. He will not allow the temptation to be more than you can stand. When you are tempted, he will show you a way out so that you can endure.* —**1 Corinthians 10:13 NLT**

We have an escort and an exit with every temptation of discord.

I want to recap and elaborate just a bit more because the consequences are so severe; we must learn all we can to guard our hearts against discord.

> *"Your love for one another will prove to the world that you are my disciples."* —**John 13:35 NLT**

Discord *(disagreement with God and conflict with others)* begins on the inside before it makes its presentation on the outside. It can be a silent, subtle pattern of ignoring the directions of the Conductor and snowball into full-blown, unapologetic rebellion.

Regardless of how it begins, if we fail to pluck out the roots of discord from our hearts, it will produce the fruit of disobedience in our lives.

Discord damages our ability to discern and respond appropriately to the voice of the Conductor because the demands of discord are recklessly aggressive. Discord partners with carnality and preferences.

And those who belong to Christ Jesus have crucified the flesh with its passions and desires. —**Galatians 5:24 ESV**

I am all too familiar with the operation of discord in my life. I have had to face some very confrontational questions from the Holy Spirit that demand a response.

Questions like, "Yolanda, do you love sleep more than you love the intentions I have for your life?" Apparently you do, because you have a pattern of disobedience when it comes to getting out of bed and praying or writing. You lie there and respond with silent disobedience."

(Ouch and oh my! Will someone dial 911? I am bleeding out over here!)

Or questions like this: "Yolanda, do you love food more than you love health? Apparently you do, because you continue to ignore the promptings to get fit, take care of your body, drink more water, eat more fiber, take vitamin supplements, and exercise."

(Help me, somebody! Call the am-bu-lance!)

Discord is a product of deception. It leads to an undisciplined life. Before long, our credibility is damaged. How credible is a morbidly obese salesperson trying to sell weight-loss products? How credible is a marriage counselor who has been divorced multiple times? How credible is a Christian who has no control of his temper, language, or emotions?

A life of discord is an undisciplined life. Our lack of discipline diminishes our influence both in the natural and spiritual realm.

In my personal examples, I learned that my silent disobedience is not silent at all, because it is loudly speaking mocking proclamations to God's intentions for my life.

My disobedience says to God, *"I am not ready for you; you are not important, your plans are optional. I will get there when I get there. I still have time. God knows my heart. I am OK; it is not that serious."*

Discord is an indication that we have lost interest and forsaken our dependency on the Conductor. We become engrossed in our solo production of living life on our terms and marching to our own rhythm.

When we live in discord we are out of step with the Spirit; so we miss our cues *(discernment)*. It shows up in our inability to know when to begin or quit a behavior, a habit, or a relationship. It diminishes our ability to discern false positives *(feeling right while believing, thinking or behaving wrong)*, causing confusion, indecisiveness, and feelings of being disoriented.

Figuratively speaking, we make the wrong sounds and ultimately destroy the harmony the Holy Spirit wants to make within our relationship with him and with others.

Let us allow this insight to provoke a determination, from this point forward, to keep our eyes and ears focused on the Conductor so that we can maintain harmony with the Spirit and others.

I remember when the Holy Spirit said to me, "Yolanda, many people are satisfied being in church but out of step. They have become *confidently comfortable* marching to their own beat—no longer able to discern the rhythm of the Spirit. The damages reach deep and wide, affecting many areas of their lives and the lives of those they were assigned to impact."

Again, allow me to reiterate: sometimes the confusion about the direction to take or the decision to make is tied to discord *(disagreement with God)*. I believe discord is at the root of discontentment, carnality, and any other struggle of the soul and spirit. In which case, we have fallen out of harmony with God by living in *disagreement* with his direction, correction, and counsel.

Again, we must be intentional about living in harmony with the Holy Spirit. At all costs, *hold the note* he gave you—*obey his instructions, and make sure your lips and lifestyle agree with His Word!* What I mean is, stay in agreement with God by practicing the principles he has prescribed in the direction, correction, and counsel of His Word.

It is worth repeating, we cannot be an effective partner with God while living in discord with His Word and in constant conflict and tension with others. At all costs, and regardless if others blatantly abandon their part, *you must hold your note.*

Harmony with God is a positioning principle. Agreement gives God access to our heart to guide, correct, and counsel us.

> *The steps of a good man are ordered by the LORD: and he delighteth in his way.* —**Psalm 37:23 KJV**

There are common *characteristics of a good man*, and the most notable is obedience. The Lord orders our steps by giving us opportunities to be obedient. He has provided His Word as a light and lamp. He sends a conviction for the purpose of course correction. He has given us the Holy Spirit for the purpose of navigation because he reveals God's intention and direction. He illuminates the who, the how and the way as a moral compass.

My God, we have everything we need to live on purpose!

So, since you and I want God's intentions to be fulfilled in our lives, no longer can we proclaim Christ and continue to live in discord.

Read it again: *"Your love for one another will prove to the world that you are my disciples."* (John 13:35 NLT).

Harmony is a product of our love for one another. God's intention is that we have credibility and that our relationships serve as proof that we are his disciples. In doing so, we become an attraction to the kingdom rather than a distraction and discredit.

God's purpose for our lives will be fulfilled within the context of relationships.

Your Thoughts on "The Danger of Discord"

Discord damages our ability to discern and respond appropriately to the voice of the Conductor because the demands of discord are recklessly aggressive.

Principle #2

Purpose Is the Master, and Zeal Is the Servant

Never be lacking in zeal, but keep your spiritual fervor, serving the Lord. —**Romans 12:11 NIV**

What I am about to say will cause all sorts of discomfort and will challenge everything you've ever been taught about purpose.

Zeal outside of the context of our relationship with the Lord is dangerous. My prayer for you and me is that the Spirit will expose the voice of carnal zeal *(driven by self-serving fleshly desires)* and destroy its influence on us.

It is God's intention for zeal to be the servant to his purpose, not the master.

If zeal were a packaged product that we could purchase, it would come with a caution label such as this:

WARNING: *Only use this product within the context of your relationship with the Lord as fuel for your spiritual fervor in serving the Lord. Any other use of this product may produce results that will jeopardize God's purpose in your life. Please use it responsibly.*

ACTIVE INGREDIENTS: *a strong feeling of passion and enthusiasm that makes users very eager or determined in their pursuit.*

Sometimes the influence of zeal is stronger than the influence of the Spirit. This happens when we spend more time daydreaming about the object of our enthusiasm than we do praying and then listening for the guidance of the Spirit. This is why we must be intentional to examine ourselves when we are *driven* toward a desired outcome.

In my experience, there have been times when my zeal for a particular thing was so strong that it diminished my discernment. Every time zeal was the master of my momentum, my ability to be led by the Spirit was diminished. As I daydreamed and fantasized about what I wanted, I grew more and more convinced that it was what God wanted for me. *(Note: The more I fantasized about it, not the more I prayed about it.)*

I remember when I was about to discharge from the Army, and I was excited about the new chapter in my life. My final assignment had been as a patient administrator at the hospital on the local military base.

As I was praying about my new career, I had decided that I wanted to become one of the administrators for an up-and-coming local medical group that had begun opening offices in our city. In fact, during my transition, I became a patient and had selected a primary physician at one of the clinics.

I could see myself there. I began daydreaming about what it would be like at my new job, leading the administration of the clinic. My zeal was so strong that it affected me physically. It happened when I was in the middle of daydreaming, and out of nowhere—I got "the goosebumps" of enthusiasm and confirmation. That's when I knew this was my job; the goosebumps were my confirmation. That was it! Now all I needed to do was take the next step and apply for the open position. My family and friends were excited for me.

Shortly after the experience, while driving, I heard the Holy Spirit so clearly: *"Stop praying about that job; I have something better."*

Wait, what? "But, Lord, the goosebumps were real. What do you mean you have something better?"

In that moment God was able to get through to me. In hindsight, the Lord rescued me from a zealous pursuit that was driving me to a destination that he had not intended for me.

What the Lord had for me was more than a job; it was a blessing. It was more than anything I could have ever imagined. The position came with favor and multiple pay increases within the first year.

Learning the difference between the blessing of the Lord and success was one of the many lessons I learned. *(I will talk more about the difference later.)* I had been so enthusiastic about the administrator job that I had missed his voice and his leadership. I had a false positive *(remember this from the previous chapter?)*. The voice of zeal was louder than the voice of the Spirit.

That's right.

The voice of zeal is very convincing. It will tell you everything you want to hear. Without discernment you can mistake the voice of zeal for the voice of the Spirit. When you echo the voice of zeal as the voice of the Spirit, you damage your credibility by misrepresenting God's mind on the matter. I compare it to you *forging God's signature*. (Read that again).

Zeal will *forge God's signature* by deceiving you to believe he has cosigned the object of your pursuit.

Prayer is a dialogue not a monologue. Practicing a lifestyle of prayer will sharpen your ability to discern the difference between the voice of the Spirit and the voice of zeal. We self-sabotage when crisis or need is the only time we press into prayer. Our unfamiliarity with his voice will make it difficult to recognize it among the many other contending voices.

Pressure and zeal can impact our ability to think clearly. Multiply that intensity, and that is the impact it has on our ability to hear the voice of the Spirit. If you make prayer a way of life, it will be easier to hear His voice under the pressure of zeal or crisis. *(Read the entire paragraph again.)*

Zeal outside of the context of our relationship with the Lord cannot be trusted. Zeal must be managed by the fruit of patience.

In your zeal, here are a couple of hard questions you should ask yourself: *Am I willing to wait and pray (rinse and repeat)? If God gives me a hard NO, will I still pursue it?*

If your zeal is unwilling to yield to patience and prayer, beware! It is out of control!

Again, it is a red flag if you are spending more time daydreaming about that pursuit or that person than you are listening and pressing into prayer about it. Warning! Warning! Your zeal is operating outside of the context of the prescribed boundary.

God wants to lead us; those that are led by the Spirit are the sons of God. Sons are led by the Spirit, not driven by zeal alone. As a Christ-follower, we must break the slave mentality that drives us to pursue things that are self-serving and counter-kingdom.

Your Thoughts on "Purpose being the Master, and Zeal being the Servant"

The voice of zeal is very convincing. It will tell you everything you want to hear.

Without discernment you can mistake the voice of zeal for the voice of the Spirit.

Enemies of Purpose

With the Lord's authority I say this: Live no longer as the Gentiles do, for they are hopelessly confused. Their minds are full of darkness; they wander far from the life God gives because they have closed their minds and hardened their hearts against him. They have no sense of shame. They live for lustful pleasure and eagerly practice every kind of impurity. —**Ephesians 4:17-19 NLT**

Ignorance is an enemy of purpose. Satan's greatest weapon is man's ignorance of God's word. Those who choose to be alienated from the life God has for them are doing so out of ignorance. The reason you are reading this book is because you are seeking, because you *care to know*. However, some know that God is the author of their purpose, and they simply don't care.

Many are content with life on their terms, unaware of what is being forfeited by not knowing and living in the *"why"* for their life.

I have experienced what I call *a second wind of stamina for living*. As I grow in the revelation of God's purposes at work in me, through me and for me, the more I am inspired to live intentionally yielded to him.

This revelation has ignited my spiritual and emotional growth and stability. I am living with an unapologetic confidence in who I am in him. I am finally living purposeful.

Another enemy of purpose is blatant disobedience because it is intended to dismantle the purposes of God in our lives. I want you to see this gem of revelation in the story of Saul and the consequences of his disobedience. We will talk more about Saul later in this chapter.

In the following passage, Samuel is reading a summary of Saul's "rap sheet" of sins:

> *"For **rebellion** is like the sin of **witchcraft**, and **stubbornness** is as iniquity and **idolatry**. Because thou hast **rejected the word of the LORD**, he hath also rejected thee from being king.*
> **—1 Samuel 15:23 KJV**

A rebellious person is a disobedient person and is being compared to a person who engages in witchcraft. Practically speaking, *witchcraft* is the act of forming an alliance with evil and leveraging the aid of the alliance to accomplish the works of evil.

In the spiritual context, my rebellion advances the kingdom of darkness and promotes the intentions of the enemy of God. A disobedient person is in partnership with the enemy and is therefore an enemy sympathizer. Enemy sympathizers do what seems right in their own eyes. They are allies with the enemy.

The process of becoming an enemy sympathizer can be subtle and happen undetected for a while until the betrayal is exposed. Before someone else other than yourself comes to mind, beware. It can happen to the best of us.

All of a sudden you find yourself agreeing and justifying ideologies that oppose God. Your attraction to old habits is renewed and, before you know it, what used to bring conviction has become a place of comfortable compromise. *(I have been here a time or two in my journey with the Lord.)*

> *People may be right in their own eyes,*
> *but the LORD examines their heart.* **—Proverbs 21:2 NLT**

Their allegiance to themselves is greater than their allegiance to God. Enemy sympathizers have a compromised heart and soon become influencers and ultimately recruiters, who champion the enemy's cause.

Living on purpose will require an unconditional allegiance to the Lord God and his principles for living. This means that you and I must recognize the strategies of the enemy and be willing to contend with our soul to surrender and obey the Lord. God measures love with the ruler of obedience.

> *Jesus replied, 'All who love me will do what I say. My Father will love them, and we will come and make our home with each of them. Anyone who doesn't love me will not obey me. And remember, my words are not my own. What I am telling you is from the Father who sent me. I am telling you these things now while I am still with you.'*
> **—John 14:23-25 NLT**

Practicing disobedience will desensitize our heart to the point we no longer feel the tension of our dissension. It is a dangerous place to be.

Purposeful living will require us to deal with misplaced allegiance to our preferences because there is no guarantee that our preference will partner with God's intentions.

So, it should not come as a surprise that God's plans are often inconsiderate of our selfish ambitions; and, certainly, our selfish ambitions are inconsiderate of God's plans.

> *But I say, walk habitually in the [Holy] Spirit [seek Him and be responsive to His guidance], and then you will certainly not carry out the desire of the sinful nature [which responds impulsively without regard for God and His precepts].* **—Galatians 5:16 AMP**

We are guilty of inviting God to our decisions even after we have rejected his counsel. Our invitation is selfish. If we experience any degree of success in our rebellious or inconsiderate choices, we equate that success with God's blessing.

Because of the deceitful nature of success, it is also an enemy of purpose. The strategy of the enemy of your soul is to offer success as an attractive incentive to living independent of God's counsel.

There is a big difference between success and blessing. A blessing is indicative that God is pleased and provoked to convey favor and reward. However, success is the advancement or achievement of an objective and can happen independent of God's good pleasure.

A blessing cannot be conveyed without God being pleased.

We must understand that God is not obligated to bless our endeavors when we refuse to consider his counsel.

<u>Good works</u> *(good deeds, religious ceremonies, and anything done in our own strength and ambition)* <u>can be dead works</u> *(works that are unable to produce or enhance spiritual life)*. This is a truth that I must be reminded of.

Success, independent of God's good pleasure, is full of dead works.

The blessing of the Lord is an intimate and sacred concept that has been reduced to a colloquial platitude and loosely affixed to dead works.

God has invited us to a partnership on his terms, not our ultimatums. God reigns supreme and will leverage the successes of anyone to accomplish his divine intention, but we must not mistake that as a blessing.

I have come to understand that my pleasures, and preferences, may lead me to places of success that are absent of the blessing of the Lord. These are places where God's purpose never intended for me to go.

We are challenged to discern the difference between the good thing and the God thing. I have learned through trial and error that purpose is not found in every good thing. In fact, distractions often come in the form of good intentions.

We must be willing to grow in our spiritual ability to navigate and recognize the familiar traps of our enemy. We are familiar with Satan's evil schemes (see 2 Corinthians 2:11).

Intimacy with God diminishes the gaps of uncertainty that exist in a platonic *(surface level)* relationship. The only way for us to grow in spiritual accuracy and discernment is to grow in our relationship with the Lord God. It takes time, intentionality, and consistency. *There are no shortcuts.*

Here are a few of my *best practices* to help you continue on this journey of learning to know his will for your life:

- **Repent** with deep sincerity for every place within you that resists and rebels against God.
- **Ask the Lord God** what he wants for your life, and expect him to lead you.
- **Value the counsel** of the Holy Spirit as if your life depends upon his leading; because it does. Since he reveals the secrets of God's heart, he can reveal the secrets of yours and help you recognize when yours is contending with him (see 1 Corinthians 2:10).

Your Thoughts on "Enemies of Purpose"

An enemy sympathizer's allegiance to themselves is greater than their allegiance to God. With their compromised heart they become influencers and recruiters who champion the enemy's cause.

The Subtlety of Disobedience

When it comes to spiritual matters, we underestimate the craftiness of our enemy and overestimate the power of our human intelligence. Our life originated in the spirit and is being contented for in both the seen and unseen world. We need the help of the Lord God to navigate both worlds.

Subtle disobedience is like being caught in an entrapment we were not expecting. When our carefree life is inconsiderate of the counsel of God, it is a setup for this entrapment. It happens when the influence of the temporary world *(the seen)* is greater than our internal, eternal spirit *(the unseen)*.

I wonder whether we have convinced ourselves that if we don't consult God then we escape the indictment of disobedience. *Absolutely not.* We are not absolved of mandatory obedience if we choose to avoid his counsel. The same applies with the stance of indifference. Indifference regarding the counsel of God is the same as disobedience.

> *But Samuel replied, "What is more pleasing to the LORD: your burnt offerings and sacrifices or your obedience to his voice? Listen! Obedience is better than sacrifice, and submission is better than offering the fat of rams. Rebellion is as sinful as witchcraft, and stubbornness as bad as worshiping idols. So because you have rejected the command of the LORD, he has rejected you as king.*
> **—1 Samuel 15:22-23 NLT**

Reading his story, it is easy to conclude that King Saul had convinced himself that his sacrifice somehow absolved him of obedience. He was known to mishandle the counsel of God, reducing it to a negotiable suggestion. He was impatient and prideful. And, to make matters worse, he was intimidated by the expectations of the people.

Can you relate? I certainly can. I have been guilty of Saul-like behavior more often than I care to admit. Help me, Lord.

We find the story in 1 Samuel 13–14. Saul was instructed to wait for Samuel to perform sacrifices in preparation for the battle with the Philistines. True to his character, Saul regarded Samuel's instructions as negotiable suggestions and chose to do what was right in his own eyes. Saul grew impatient. Samuel was taking too long to return, so Saul took matters into his own hands. Rather than wait for his assignment, he chose to perform a good thing with a disobedient heart.

When Samuel returned, he wasted no time rebuking Saul's disobedience. Before moving on, I need you to see yourself in Saul's story, so that you can recognize and contend with your Saul-like tendencies.

I was speaking to a group of ladies that I meet with regularly and shared this provocative thought:

Anyone who thinks that there is an acceptable substitute to obedience is delusional. Anyone who thinks that their substitute has no impact on their effectiveness, spiritual influence, and authority, they are deceived. Perhaps this is the result of practicing disobedience for so long; the ability to feel the tension in their soul and spirit has been lost.

Have you ever come to a contaminated conclusion that God was taking too long to do what you wanted him to do, so you took matters into your own hands? Did you then expect him to celebrate your success, or rescue you from your failure?

Have you ever buckled to the pressure to please or impress people, and it led to your disregard for the counsel of the Lord?

The wrong perspective of waiting on God will make us weary in well doing, and eventually we will faint and default to disobedience.

The proper perspective of waiting on God is packed with renewed strength and stamina from the Spirit. In other words, your wait is accompanied by supernatural help. *This is so encouraging to me.*

> *<u>They that wait upon the L<small>ORD</small></u> shall <u>renew their strength</u>; they shall <u>mount up</u> with wings as eagles; <u>they shall run</u>, and not be weary; and <u>they shall walk</u>, and not faint.* —**Isaiah 40:31 KJV**

Without a revelation of the character and intentions of God toward those whom he loves, those who wait will lack the grace and stamina that only comes from waiting upon him *(rest and trust in the Lord)*.

Saul offered a substitute for obedience. You would think that doing a good thing even in the wrong timing would be acceptable. *Think again.* God's instructions are not suggestions; therefore, even Saul's seemingly good thing done in disobedience was rejected by God.

Your sacrifice of time and money is no substitute for obedience. A good thing is regarded by God as an evil thing if it is done in disobedience.

When Saul won the battle against the Philistines, despite his disregard for Samuel's instructions, it appears that his disobedience was rewarded. It looks like he got away with it.

I will say it again: we are deceived if we think for one moment that God gives us a pass, allowing us to escape the consequences of disobedience. We don't have the capacity to know the perpetual impact of one act of disobedience.

In 1 Samuel 15, the Lord gave Saul another opportunity to obey the commandment to destroy the entire tribe of the Amalekites. The Lord said to kill everyone and everything. It was God's intention to make good on his promise to blot out the remembrance of the Amalekites because of their relentless actions against God's people (see 1 Samuel 15).

History tells us that when the children of Israel left Egypt, the Amalekites launched ferocious attacks, destroying their farms and homes, and torturing their women and children. They even forced the parents to watch as they murdered their infants.

Once again, Saul negotiated God's commandments as though they were suggestions. He did what seemed right in his own eyes, choosing to spare Agag, the Amalekite king, and everything that he found appealing, including the best of the livestock.

Saul expected God and Samuel to be impressed. Pride, rebellion, and idolatry made him delusional concerning the gravity of his disobedience. *"To obey is better than sacrifice,"* Samuel said to King Saul (see 1 Samuel 15:22 KJV).

Have you ever convinced yourself that God will be satisfied with your substitute for full obedience *(like you are doing him a favor; like a he-can-take-it-or-leave-it kind of attitude)*? Help us, Lord!

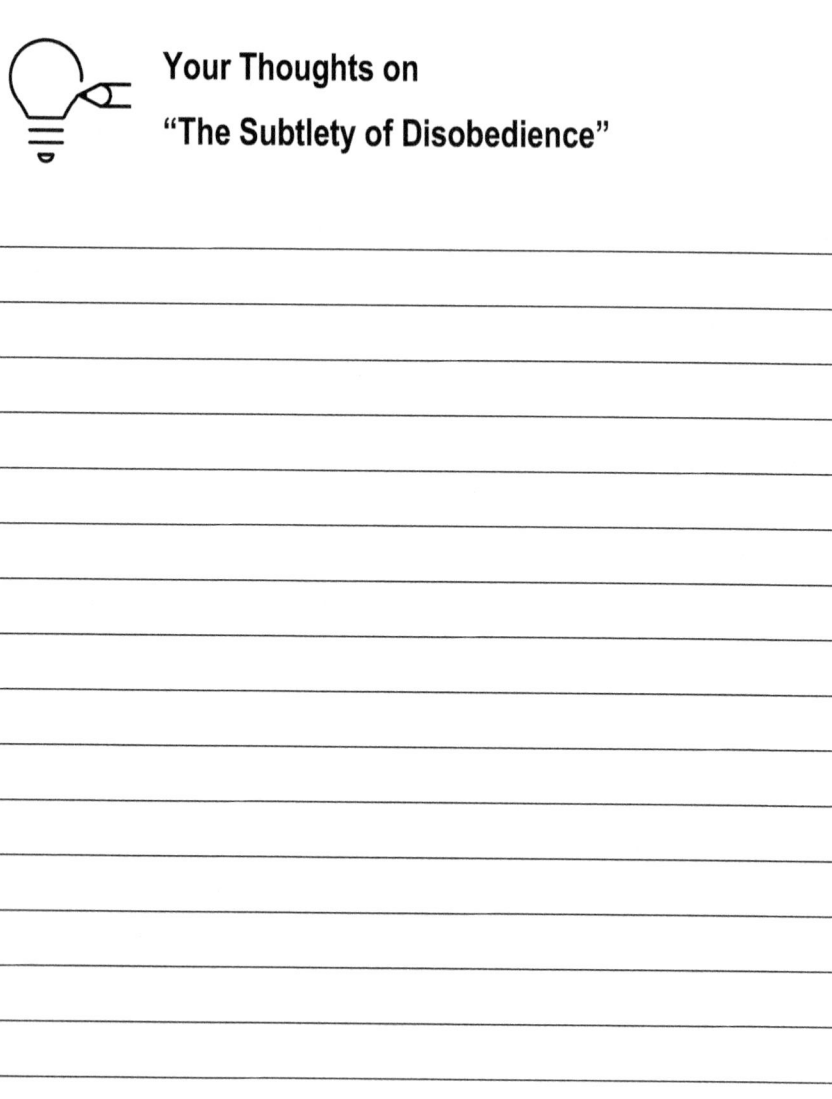

Your Thoughts on "The Subtlety of Disobedience"

When it comes to spiritual matters, we underestimate the craftiness of our enemy and overestimate the power of our human intelligence.

Comfortable Resistance

We have become so comfortable rejecting God's commandments and council that we no longer feel the tension of our resistance. In doing so, we are reinforcing an alliance with the enemy of our soul when we should be denouncing every counter-kingdom alliance.

> *So humble yourselves before God. Resist the devil, and he will flee from you.* —**James 4:7 NLT**

Comfortable resistance is a sure sign that we have become intoxicated by our perspective. I believe it begins with a little resistance here and there until we progress to blatant disregard for the Lord's counsel and commandments. This is when our convictions are eclipsed by the preferences of our dark, toxic soul.

By natural wiring, we present prideful resistance by insisting that God meet us in the middle for the purpose of negotiation. We expect him to compromise his requirement for total obedience in exchange for a substitute of our choosing.

If we are honest with ourselves, we are as foolish as Saul, who pridefully justified his resistance by boldly offering sacrifices as a substitute.

Pride and preference are at the root of our resistance. We idolize our intelligence. We think we know better than the omniscient God.

Mankind is the only creature that resists God. Our audacity is astonishing, considering that the elements and all other living creatures obey God. Yet the one he created in his image and likeness, and the one he chose to have a relationship with, offers the fiercest resistance. Help us, Lord!

Pride and preferences will influence what we are willing to surrender. This is why we tend to offer a substitute rather than our obedience.

Pride makes disobedience comfortable by devaluing and silencing God's counsel. Resistance to God's council should never be comfortable.

A yielded life will require us to conquer our prideful proclivity to offer substitutes for obedience.

Your Thoughts on "Comfortable Resistance"

We have become so comfortable rejecting God's commandments and council that we no longer feel the tension of our resistance.

Generational Impact

Fast forward to the book of Esther, and we see how King Saul's disobedience impacted many generations. Saul hoped his sacrifice would be an acceptable substitute; however, the consequences were generational.

We grossly *underestimate* the generational impact of our disobedience, and we *overestimate* the power of our zeal to lead us to the purposes of God. Like Saul, we are prone to run reckless and zealous without any consultation from the Spirit of God.

We must understand that every act of disobedience is a big deal and could have perpetual consequences.

We cannot comprehend the future impact of a present moment of disobedience. Saul's decision to spare King Agag preserved his descendants, allowing them to multiply for six centuries. Nearly 500 years later, Saul's actions forced all his descendants, including Mordecai and Esther, to contend with what he was commanded to destroy. Despite Saul's disobedience, God had a plan to redeem the children of Israel.

Haman was a descendant of King Agag, and he hated the Jews. Assuming he knew the history between the Amalekites and the Jews, he had reason to hate them. He conspired to kill them all, but God had other plans for Mordecai and Esther.

In the story, we see the perpetual effect of Saul's disobedience. God rejected Saul as king, which means Saul's disobedience was expensive, costing him his position of authority.

After Samuel sorely rebuked him, he visited Saul no more. Saul lost the access and influence of the prophetic voice of that day. This meant he was at a disadvantage for divine strategies, wisdom, answers, solutions, and everything that the voice of the Spirit provides.

Ultimately Saul was killed by an Amalekite, a descendant of the king he was instructed to kill.

We can learn a few timeless lessons from Saul that will be valuable keys for purposeful living. First, we all must raise our reverence for the word of the Lord whether it comes in the form of prophecy, correction, instructions, or encouragement.

Like Saul, we are prone to mishandling the commandments of the Lord, regarding them as suggestions to be negotiated, tampered with, or tailored to suit our comfortability. We reason with his word until we reason our way into deception and disobedience.

Instead, we must be quick to hear and obey (James 1:19). When we are slow to hear and agree with God, or when we offer a substitute for obedience, it indicates dullness of hearing and spiritual immaturity (Hebrews 5:11).

The spiritually immature will discard the eternally significant things in exchange for temporary pleasure. Obedience has eternal significance, and disobedience has eternal consequences. *(Read that again.)*

Diminished authority is one of many consequences of underestimating the value of the word of the Lord. This makes for a frustrating experience when attempting to practice spiritual principles without the necessary authority, and they don't work. Recurring failures cause us to question our faith and the validity of the principles.

Here is a sobering thought: the voice of authority that we have practiced ignoring is the same voice that we seek to intervene in our crisis or satisfy our selfish petitions. Whew!

Disobedience will also dull our sensitivity to the prophetic voices in our life. *Samuel visited Saul no more.* Practically speaking, *prophetic voices* as words spoken by the inspiration of the Holy Spirit in the form of a revelation, instructions or wisdom for the present or the future. The prophetic is a source of strategies, answers, impartation and so much more.

You can be in the room where the Spirit is moving and speaking and miss it entirely because you have lost the ability to know and hear. We need the prophetic operating in us and around us because we are at a serious disadvantage without it.

Again, the very thing that God had commanded Saul to destroy was what destroyed him.

Paul says, *"For if ye live after the flesh, ye shall die: but if ye through the Spirit do mortify the deeds of the body, ye shall live."* (Romans 8:13 KJV).

I remember an incident while serving in San Antonio, Texas. I was sincerely wrong, but God arrested me and turned my heart toward his intention.

(This, right here, is a place for a prayer pause: *Lord, for the sake of thy kingdom, please arrest me when I am headed in the wrong direction yet fully persuaded that I have made the right choice. Open my eyes to see you that I may turn toward your intention. Amen.*)

At the time I was a Captain, attending one of my career courses required for promotion. The course was nearly over, and the time had come for us to receive our next assignment. The memory is still fresh, like it was yesterday.

There I was, standing in the temporary office with the career advisor when he informed me of my next assignment. I was assigned to Fort Campbell, Kentucky. *What do you mean Fort Campbell?* I knew I did not want to go to Fort Campbell and I let my advisor know what I thought. I told him, *"I am not going to Fort Campbell. I need you to find me another assignment because I am not going!"*

That's when it happened. I was arrested—by the Holy Spirit.

The Holy Spirit stopped me in my tracks: *"You will accept that assignment to Fort Campbell."* That is all I remember about it. I waited for the opportunity to peep my head back into the office to let the counselor know. *"I will take that assignment to Fort Campbell, sir, and thank you."* I wonder what he was thinking after how I had just behaved. I wonder if he thought, *"This crazy Captain may need to make a pit stop for a mental evaluation before she goes anywhere else."*

Thank you, Lord, for arresting me in my selfish decision and turning my heart toward your intention.

This book is a product of the generational impact of purpose, tied to that act of obedience. In fact, the divine connections and seemingly random daily dealings of our lives make up the wonderful tapestry of purpose in the life of a believer.

If we want to live on purpose, it will require many sacrifices and selfless decisions. It will require us to seek harmony. We will have to contend with our carnal zeal to pursue pleasure and preferences. It will demand that we either die to our flesh, or risk forfeiture of a life filled with God's intention. We get to choose.

The quality of life for future generations will be impacted by whether we *choose to die*. It bears repeating that living on purpose requires a toe tag.

I am thankful that our disobedience never positions God at a disadvantage. He is ahead of us by eternity. His plans, strategies, and solutions originated and existed in eternity before the problems existed in time.

When we read the story in the book of Esther we see the grace of God at work through Mordecai and Esther. Saul's disobedience had put them in a predicament that only obedience could deliver them from.

Sometimes the fastest way out of a predicament is to obey our way out. Mordecai and Esther fasted, prayed, and obeyed the commands of the Lord and delivered an entire nation from destruction.

Haman was hung on the gallows that he prepared for Mordecai. God's people were saved from the intentions of the enemy. Mordecai was promoted and received Haman's property, and Esther became queen and was highly favored by the king and the Persian people.

Obedience saved and redeemed generations.

If we are unwilling to conquer and destroy the enemies of purpose in our generation, they will contend with the purpose of future generations. I can't help but wonder whether the deterioration of the moral fiber our generation or the unrevealed strategies and solutions for the world problems we face are a result of the disobedience of previous generations.

Purposeful living will require that we soberly consider the perpetual impact of our disobedience.

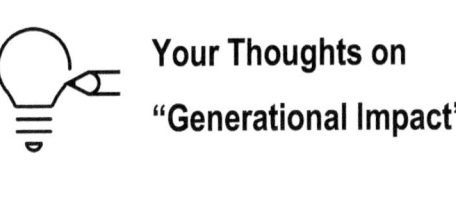

Your Thoughts on "Generational Impact"

The quality of life for future generations will be impacted by whether we choose to die. It bears repeating that living on purpose requires a toe tag.

PRINCIPLE #3

Purpose Serves the King's Pleasure

And he hath on his vesture and on his thigh a name written, KING OF KINGS, AND LORD OF LORDS. —**Revelation 19:16 KJV**

In the passage, John the revelator gives us an account of his supernatural experience while on the Isle of Patmos. He is describing a vision of our Lord Jesus, the King of kings, and Lord of lords.

As we understand the absolute sovereignty *(dominion, self-governing independence)* of God, our carnal-minded *(fleshly, sensual)* theories about purpose will unravel.

Purpose was never about me getting what I want out of life, but has always been all about me serving the King's good pleasure. *"Seek the Kingdom of God above all else, and live righteously, and he will give you everything you need"* (Matthew 6:33 NLT).

Sometimes the intention of a passage can be lost in translation; and if we are familiar with the passage, we don't bother reaching for the deeper meaning. This is one of those passages that I want to take the time to excavate the deeper meaning.

The Bible is a compilation of multiple writers who were inspired by the Spirit to record their experience with the Word of God.

> *In the beginning was the Word, and the Word was with God, and the Word was God. . . The Word became flesh and made his dwelling among us.* —**John 1:1, 14 NIV**

Although there are many translations of the Scriptures, the common thread of the Scriptures is the revelation of Jesus Christ, the Word made flesh. There are patterns, symbols, parables, and cultural references that are not to be ignored because of their deeper meaning and practical application for you and me.

For instance, between the Old and New Testament scriptures, there are more than eighty references to the "kingdom." The teachings of Jesus Christ were centered on the kingdom of God.

Jesus, *The Word made flesh* was also a political figure dwelling among men. One of his many objectives in the process of fulfilling scriptures was to establish his kingdom.

> *"Nor will people say, 'Look! Here it is!' or, 'There it is!' For the kingdom of God is among you [because of My presence].*
> —**Luke 17:21 AMP**

Seeking the kingdom first is a life that places the King's good pleasure above our own. When we do, it will change our perspectives and our priorities, and posture us for his highest purposes.

Here is the promise in this passage that I want you to see. When his good pleasure becomes the object of our affection, the intimate relationship gives us access to everything we need. He is speaking not only of the essentials of life that are temporary but also of the eternal intangibles that each of us desperately needs. I need peace of mind. I need strategies and solutions. I need revelation of God himself. I need healing and wholeness. I need grace and mercy. *Do you get the picture?*

Old Testament scholar Graeme Goldsworthy summarized the kingdom of God when he wrote, "God's people in God's place [wherever you are] under God's rule."

This spiritual kingdom on the inside of us is to reflect the eternal kingdom, in that it is a place where God reigns supreme. Kingdom-centered living is a life that is in harmony with God.

God's purpose for our lives is intended to complement, support, and expand his kingdom, not our own empire. When we live for the temporary pleasures of this life, we are a liability and threat to the influence of His kingdom.

I believe one reason many suffer in varying types of chaos and confusion is because they live in pursuit of the temporary. Jesus promises to take care of both our temporary and eternal needs, if we prioritize the will of the King and his kingdom.

> *I have meat to eat that ye know not of. . ... My meat is to do the will of him that sent me, and to finish his work.*
> **—John 4:32-34 KJV**

Jesus is referring to the will of God as spiritual meat and the source of his spiritual nourishment. From this one passage we learn that there is a sustaining supply of strength and stamina for life, found in doing the will of God.

This is the disconnect for many who are emotionally fatigued and prone to experiment with varying strategies in the hopes of discovering their identity or sense of value and purpose. Many who seemingly have it all are void inside.

It is a painful reality that many are choosing suicide as an escape because their search for answers has only resulted in more questions. So many are looking for purpose and hope in all the wrong places.

This is why I am moved with such compassion; I am willing to spend my life sharing these principles of purpose that have forever changed my life.

**Your Thoughts on
"Purpose Serves the King's Pleasure"**

God's purpose for our lives is intended to complement, support, and expand his kingdom, not our own empire.

Kingdom-centered Prayer

> *Our Father which art in heaven, Hallowed be thy name.* **Thy kingdom come, Thy will** *be done in earth, as it is in heaven.*
> —**Matthew 6:9-10 KJV**

We have been given stewardship of the purposes of God. The trust that is conveyed in stewardship should provoke honor.

In this pattern for prayer, Jesus teaches his disciples to first put the Father in proper perspective. *Hallowed* means his name is holy, sanctified, and set apart. There is no other god beside our God. The next order is to pray that the *will of our God* becomes the prevailing will in the earth.

The will of the Father on the earth happens through us. We cannot accomplish his will if we insist on living our way on our terms based upon our preferences.

Our assignment is to expand his kingdom on the earth by living a life yielded to his authority and priorities. When we do, others are drawn to do the same; and God's intentions are fulfilled.

Our daily question should be, "What does the King require of me today?"

I want to use Esther's story again because I appreciate how it provides a powerful illustration of this principle. In the story, the king was seeking to replace his wife, Vashti, who through rebellious behavior, had embarrassed the king to the point of shame.

King Ahasuerus ordered that all the fair young virgins be brought to the palace at Shushan for purification. This was the process required to prepare them to go before the king as a candidate for queen.

It was the custom for the woman to choose how she wanted to be adorned for her presentation to the king. True to the custom, the women made their selection without inquiry or consideration of the king's preferences. For them, it was personal, but Esther had a different strategy.

When it was time for her (Esther) to go to the king's palace, she was given her choice of whatever clothing or jewelry she wanted to take from the harem. —**Esther 2:13 NLT**

The chamberlain was a post of honor and had influence with the king. The chamberlain was a trusted source for insight regarding the king's preferences. In other words, he knew what the king liked.

When it was Esther's turn to go to the king, she accepted the advice of Hegai, the eunuch in charge of the harem. She asked for nothing except what he suggested, and she was admired by everyone who saw her. —**Esther 2:15 NLT**

Esther understood something about the king and his kingdom. She knew that the king's preference should take priority above her own. She knew that the only way to be certain of what might please the king was to consult the one who knew the king better than anyone in the kingdom—the chamberlain.

The Holy Spirit is our chamberlain living on the inside of us.

But it was to us that God revealed these things by his Spirit. For his Spirit searches out everything and shows us God's deep secrets. No one can know a person's thoughts except that person's own spirit, and no one can know God's thoughts except God's own Spirit. And we have received God's Spirit (not the world's spirit), so we can know the wonderful things God has freely given us.
—**1 Corinthians 2:10-12 NLT**

We can know what pleases God, and we should want to know.

I owe an enormous debt of gratitude to the late Dr. Myles Munroe. He was a prolific writer on the topic of purpose. He gave us such wisdom and insight in his writings and messages.

Dr. Munroe wrote, "For many believers, prayer does not work the way it should because they have made it a religious exercise of pleading for a favor rather than a legal act of asserting their rights and privileges as Kingdom citizens. Prayer is business with the government of God" (*God's Big Idea: Reclaiming God's Original Purpose in Your Life,* Destiny Image Publishers, 2008). When we petition the King properly, we are only asking for what He has already promised.

This insight has changed my prayer life in a radical way. The Holy Spirit is teaching me that my faith is not a wand that I wave when I want to secure a favorable outcome to my prayer. My faith's greatest purpose is to secure the proper perspective of God's will, so then my prayers can be leveraged to accomplish it.

Why is this important? Because sometimes our prayers are provoked by our preferences and selfish perspective rather than our desire to see the will of the king. To avoid the inevitable frustration that results from self-centered prayer, we must accept that God is not obligated to honor prayers when they don't complement his intentions.

I will say it again: The purpose of prayer has never been to obtain our will, but the will of the king. *It will take time to wrap our minds around this principle.*

I have begun praying that the will of heaven will influence my life and relationships in my present, in my future, and in the world around me. I have learned that kingdom-centered prayers are one of the best ways to partner with God's intentions. *(This has been a next-level revelation for me.)*

When we petition God for *his will* to take the leading role in our lives, we are inviting *his intentions* to reign supreme and influence everything about our lives.

Purpose is not mine to claim as my own; it has belonged, and forever will belong, to the King. What audacity it takes for me, the creature, to even think I am intelligent enough to dictate and determine my own purpose! Wow, I had so much to unlearn.

As a child I was taught, "You can be anything you want to be when you grow up." We have changed the language, but the message was the same. Well-meaning people taught us that we were in control and can define our purpose. So, for many years, I lived confused and discouraged, trying to *figure out how to figure it out*.

I understand the intention to encourage and empower our children to be ambitious and set goals in life. However, this type of generational advice desensitizes our children to the importance of yielding to God's purpose by encouraging them to make life plans without the counsel of the wonderful counselor (Isaiah 9:6).

> *For unto us a child is born, unto us a son is given: and the government shall be upon his shoulder: and his name shall be called Wonderful, Counsellor, The mighty God, The everlasting Father, The Prince of Peace.* —**Isaiah 9:6 KJV**

I do not remember ever being taught that God has a plan for my life and that I should seek His help to follow it.

> *For the kingdom of God is not a matter of eating and drinking, but of righteousness, peace and joy in the Holy Spirit.*
> —**Romans 14:17 NIV**

We must replace these popular lessons with the message of the kingdom. Purpose is only found in relationship with the King.

We must encourage our children to be filled with the Spirit so that they can be everything God intended. We must assure them that he will order their steps along the way. May we convince them by our own example that his plans are far more rewarding than their greatest ambitions.

Your Thoughts on "Kingdom-centered Prayer"

Our daily question should be, "What does the King require of me today?"

We can know what pleases God, and we should want to know.

Purpose is not mine to claim as my own; it has belonged, and forever will belong, to the King.

Get in Step

If we live by the Spirit, let us also keep in step with the Spirit.
—**Galatians 5:25 ESV**

Priscilla Shirer, a widely recognized actress, evangelist, and *New York Times* best-selling author, gave this illustration about Michael Jackson, and it fits so well with our conversation:

Michael Jackson was arguably the greatest entertainer that ever lived. In a story about the production of the music video for the song "Billy Jean," on the *Thriller* album, it was reported that the producer warned Michael that his freestyle steps were out of synch with the pre-programmed light panels.

If you remember the video, as Michael walked, the panels on the ground lit up in perfect sync with his steps. The producer warned that because the panels had been pre-programmed, he needed to stay in step to accomplish the intention of the production.

Michael's spontaneous performance was out of step with the producer's intention. No doubt Michael wanted a well-produced video; however, the objective could not be achieved if he refused to stay in step with what the producer had planned. He may have enjoyed himself, but the final product would have been an epic failure.

The sinful nature wants to do evil, which is just the opposite of what the Spirit wants. And the Spirit gives us desires that are the opposite of what the sinful nature desires. These two forces are constantly fighting each other, so you are not free to carry out your good intentions. —**Galatians 5:17 NLT**

Our soul *(mind, will, emotions, intellect)* will work overtime to lure us away from God's will by making our will appear more appealing and rewarding. This has been the place of tension since Adam and Eve's deception.

Our soul works to convince us that God is withholding something that is achievable if we outwit him. *(Doesn't that sound absurd?)* We are torn between the desire to please God, and the temptation to choose our way. But when we are yielded, the Spirit is able to work within us to <u>*will and to do*</u> what pleases God. The Spirit gives the *want to* and the power to follow through (see Philippians 2:13).

Let's seek the kingdom before we choose our brilliant life plans, and set sail to accomplish them.

Now in a large house there are not only vessels and objects of gold and silver, but also vessels and objects of wood and of earthenware, and some are for honorable (noble, good) use and some for dishonorable (ignoble, common). Therefore, if anyone cleanses himself from these things [which are dishonorable—disobedient, sinful], he will be a vessel for honor, sanctified [set apart for a special purpose and], useful to the Master, prepared for every good work. — **2 Timothy 2:20-21 (AMP)**

Without the help of the Holy Spirit, it is impossible to stay in step. The only way to fulfill the King's highest purpose is for us to be willing to abandon our greatest ambitions; that's what it takes to get in step.

Your Thoughts on "Get in Step"

Without the help of the Holy Spirit, it is impossible to stay in step.

The only way to fulfill the King's highest purpose is for us to be willing to abandon our greatest ambitions; that's what it takes to get in step.

Repentance Is a Kingdom Strategy

"From that time Jesus began to preach, saying, 'Repent, for the kingdom of heaven is at hand.'" —**Matthew 4:17 ESV**

Repentance is a kingdom strategy for wilderness wanderers *(the lost)* and kingdom dwellers who are *living in step with the Spirit*, because all are prone to wander. If we are not intentional to practice repentance, our sinful nature will construct blinders on our eyes and calluses on our heart, and leave us desensitized to the Spirit, wandering in the wilderness.

True repentance happens when we change our minds about sin, choosing to agree with what God says about it. Repentance is a kingdom strategy that places God in the right perspective. It is a posture of humility, and it attracts God's grace and favor.

The importance of living a repentant life cannot be overstated. In fact, we don't talk about it enough; and when we do, we dilute the message, valuing comfortability over transformation. We stop just shy of transformation, which is the fruit of conviction.

When we are living yielded, it is easier to detect empathy toward sin. It can happen to *anyone;* and when it does, repentance is the right response for *everyone.*

Sin is the fruit of temptation and deception, and the consummation of disagreement with God. Practicing sin will deter us from his purpose. Consequently, it is impossible to be influenced by what we refuse to agree with. *(Ouch!)*

We are partners with God which means we have *kingdom business* to tend to. So we must shift our paradigm so we can live in the revelation that purpose is all about fulfilling his kingdom plans and not our selfish objectives.

Paul wrote that our body is the temple of the Holy Spirit. The word comes from the Latin *templum*, meaning *"consecrated piece of ground" or "a building for worship."*

Repentance is how we *consecrate* our heart for Him to rule and reign. Repentance enables us to refocus and reinforce the terms of our partnership. As we grow in our understanding and consistency, we will become a more honorable and impactful partner.

Honor in our partnership with the Spirit will become more consistent when it is based upon what we *know*, rather than what we think, feel or what we have been told.

In the culture of the biblical scribes, *to know* was the equivalent of *to do, to perform or to complete or consummate.*

Other translations of the same word refer to *intimacy*.

When we *know* a truth, we should <u>act, reflect, and reproduce the likeness of what we *know*.</u> In our modern culture, *to know* is loosely translated to imply *an awareness of information and the freedom to choose or reject it.*

The Holy Spirit wants to reveal truth to us so that our lives can reflect what he has revealed. Purposeful living will require our lives to reflect what the Spirit reveals.

Now that my process of learning to know his will has begun, my prayers are different. *Lord, may what I say that I know demand the corresponding action that pleases you. Lord, may what I know soak beyond my mind to the deepest recesses of my soul and spirit and change me. Lord, purge me from every preference that opposes your intentions. Lord, deliver me from every determination that deters me from your desires. Lord, may your purpose in my life be the portion that satisfies and fulfills me. May it soothe my soul, and may it be the answer to all my questions and the counter to every one of my excuses.*

At this point I pray you are beginning to see, what the Spirit is attempting to reveal about your value and purpose.

He will use the smallest details about my life to complement his kingdom-sized purpose. I understand that I must be able to discern and deal with anything or anyone that presents a compromise or conflict to my assignments. I must leverage my career, education, skills, experience, relationships, finances, and influence to help me be the best partner in this kingdom business.

Everything and everyone must be kept in proper perspective, otherwise they can capture our attention, distort our discernment, and detour us from his intentions.

I can no longer be satisfied with knowing and refuse to render the proper response. This passive awareness will no longer satisfy. In other words, I have been provoked by the Holy Spirit with a bold intolerance for behavior that contends with his Kingdom-sized purpose.

When I am in discord *(disagreement with God and conflict with others)* the discomfort in my spirit is nearly unbearable, and it doesn't take long for me to feel the urgency to repent and reconcile back to a place of agreement with God.

I have learned the importance of practicing repentance. It is a powerful kingdom strategy. Repent, because the Kingdom of God is at hand. In other words, there is Kingdom business to accomplish and repentance exposes and diminishes any empathy when may have for sin. Sin in our life hinders our effectiveness in the Kingdom partnership.

**Your Thoughts on
"Repentance Is a Kingdom Strategy"**

When we are living yielded, it is easier to detect empathy toward sin.

It can happen to anyone; and when it does, repentance is the right response for everyone.

PRINCIPLE #4

Purpose Is Eternal

For we are God's handiwork, created in Christ Jesus to do good works, which God prepared in advance for us to do.
—**Ephesians 2:10 NIV**

"Where purpose is not known, abuse is inevitable."
—**Dr. Myles Munroe**

This is one of my all-time favorite quotes. I believe Dr. Myles Munroe got this straight from the heart of God. We see the consequences of self-defined purpose and the desperation of those lost and wandering, still trying to figure it out.

You cannot *unhear or unread* what Paul wrote in 1 Corinthians 6:19-20—we don't belong to ourselves. The realization that we do not belong to ourselves should provoke us to repent and humble us to a place of surrender to the Author of our purpose.

For as by one man's disobedience many were made sinners, so by the obedience of one shall many be made righteous.
—**Romans 5:19 KJV**

Redeem the Time

Ephesians 5:15-18 (NLT) says, "*So be careful how you live. Don't live like fools, but like those who are wise. Make the most of every opportunity in these evil days. Don't act thoughtlessly, but understand what the Lord wants you to do. Don't be drunk with wine, because that will ruin your life. Instead, be filled with the Holy Spirit."*

This book is a product of God's intention for my life. I wrote it in obedience. I had to push past every feeling of inadequacy to complete this book. I thought that, if I could live my life as a good Christian and never write another book, I would be just fine, but God said, I am an author of many books. So let God be true and everyone else, including my fickle emotions, be a liar. I have resolved that I will live yielded and in agreement with what I know about his intentions for my life. Time is of the essence.

What is the next step for you? When will you resolve to live yielded?

The Greek word for *redeem* means *"to purchase from ransom, to rescue from loss."* It is not too late to live yielded and *redeem* the lost time.

It is time to sober up from being intoxicated with the preference of independence and selfish living. God stands ready and willing to partner with you no matter where you are or what you have done with your life up to this point.

You get to decide how you will respond to what the Spirit is revealing to you.

From Genesis to Revelation, the Bible is filled with stories of God partnering with sons of God to accomplish his purpose in the earth. I realized that his partners included former liars, murderers, blasphemers, adulterers, and cowards. Honestly, I was encouraged by the pattern of flawed partners. It meant there was hope for me as I am *learning to know* his will for my life.

The invitation of partnership with God to reconcile the world back to himself is extended to everyone. *(Read that again.)* *"For we are laborers together with God: ye are God's husbandry, ye are God's building."* (1 Corinthians 3:9 KJV).

Now you know too much to continue living foolishly. Living kingdom-centered is to reject the world's way of thinking and live by more superior principles. You are on the earth to be an agent of impact for the kingdom of light. *(Read that again.)* Note these words from apostle Paul:

> *Imitate God, therefore, in everything you do, because you are his dear children. Live a life filled with love, following the example of Christ. He loved us and offered himself as a sacrifice for us, a pleasing aroma to God.* —**Ephesians 5:1-2 NLT**

You can be the agent of impact and begin living Kingdom-centered today. It is an urgent and absolute necessity because we are running out of time. The character of God is on trial every day and the world is deceived, calling wrong, right and right, wrong.

Modern culture despises the holy things and worships the things that defile the body, soul, and spirit. We can be the example they need so they can discover what purposeful living looks like.

Purposeful living has little to do with a big house, a luxury car, or lots of friends and money, although these things can be a blessing. However, if I allow anything or anyone to dictate my pursuit, it is a distraction to God's intentions for my life.

I know too much to remain distracted. I am determined to be sober until God says I am finished.

Although in the process of writing this book, I struggled with undisciplined habits of procrastination, misguided zeal and misaligned priorities, I finished it. In the process I learned that if I prioritize the assignments, he would provide the grace to accomplish my tasks that I often allow to take precedence.

My Kingdom assignments have eternal significance, but the impact of my tasks are temporary at best. It has required me to sacrifice time with my family and postpone many pleasures and preferences. However, I am convinced I was born to write this book.

Now that this assignment is complete, are you ready to harmonize by agreeing with the principles shared in the pages? This book is a sound that God has allowed me to release in time.

I pray that the ears of the willing will hear and begin harmonizing with me as they learn to know his will for their lives.

Instead, we will speak the truth in love, growing in every way more and more like Christ, who is the head of his body, the church. He makes the whole body fit together perfectly. As each part does its own special work, it helps the other parts grow, so that the whole body is healthy and growing and full of love.
—Ephesians 4:15-16 NLT

One of the principles God set in motion is our dependency upon one another to fulfill his intentions. Since people are the object of His love and the vessels he has chosen to fulfil his purpose, let's be intentional to encourage one another to redeem the time.

We don't have an eternity to fulfil his intentions through us in time. Furthermore, the way I see it, we are behind and are in desperate need to redeem the time.

I am optimistic that we can redeem the time by applying and sharing the insights from this *little book about purpose*. I believe God will reconcile individuals, families, relationships, and even generations. That's what I call the exponential potential of *purpose* at work.

**Your Thoughts on
"Purpose Is Eternal: Redeem the Time"**

Above everything that we could live for, our purpose is to partner with God to reconcile the world back to himself.

Perpetual Grace

"Grace is free sovereign favor to the ill-deserving" (B. B. Warfield).

The story in Acts 9 tells of Paul *(Saul)* becoming a follower of Jesus after his encounter on the road into Damascus. On the same road that he traveled with the wrong intention, God met him through an appointment with his eternally significant purpose.

God knows where we are. He can find and arrest us with his presence. I am so glad he arrested Paul. I want you to see that Paul was sincerely wrong, but God leveraged his unrighteous commitment to perpetuate his eternally significant purpose.

Paul had been on his way from Jerusalem to Syria Damascus, with permission from the high priest to seek out and arrest followers of Jesus. The plan was to return them to Jerusalem as prisoners for questioning and possible execution.

God chose to blind Paul in order to reveal himself. In Paul's blindness, he heard and obeyed God's instructions. This is one of the most profound pictures of perpetual grace I have ever read about.

Paul was sincerely wrong, on his way to fulfill unrighteous intentions when the Lord rescued him from his deception and used blindness as a process to open his spiritual eyes. *God's ways are beyond comprehension.*

Maybe our greatest revelation in life is tied to our response to him in our "blind spots" *(areas where we do not have all the answers)*. We must listen and discern the instructions of the Spirit and obey. His grace is sufficient to reveal truth, especially in the blind spots of life.

Sometimes we are sincerely wrong in our direction. But when purpose speaks, the grace of God will allow a yielded heart to hear and discern. Our proper response to grace will always lead to a conversion or course correction. Have you ever paused to think what the condition of the church would be like if Paul had rejected God's intentions on the road to Damascus?

Immediately following his conversion, Paul began boldly proclaiming Jesus as the Messiah, which made him a target of the Jewish leaders who now wanted to kill him. The believers in the city thought the best way to save his life was to send him away. So, he got into a large basket, and they lowered him out of a window to escape (Acts 9). The obedience of the believers in 40 AD was a platform for God's eternal purpose in Paul's life.

Furthermore, because purpose has its origin in eternity, it is not bound by time nor by any other temporary thing. Catch this: every past, present and future believer is a beneficiary of the perpetual grace and God's eternal purpose at work in Paul.

There was more than a bold, radical new convert in the basket that day. Nearly half of the New Testament scriptures were in the basket. Every life that has been, is being, or will be nourished by the Spirit-inspired scriptures penned by Paul was in the basket.

I always say that the benefits of obedience are perpetual. They cannot be quantified because many generations are the potential bounty of our obedience, or the casualties of our disobedience.

Again, obedience is a compass God uses to charter his intentions for our lives.

Furthermore, the DNA of purpose is found in every step of obedience.

So then, who can measure the exponential impact?

If I could have a conversation with the apostle Paul, I would say this: *"Apostle Paul, thank you for your obedience. Because of your obedience, my children's children will read your writings, gain the proper perspective of God, and be reconciled unto him. I appreciate your ministry."*

Now that we have a better understanding of the exponential potential of purpose, may we never again underestimate the impact of our obedience.

Now we are equipped.

Now we are weaponized with insight and a deeper revelation.

We will no longer be deceived by a pursuit, instead we will choose to yield.

The enemy of our soul wishes I had never written this book, and that you had never read it. I know he hates the fact that you finished it and were not deterred by my unconventional writing style and antics.

Hell is in an uproar by your firm decision to render the proper response to what the Spirit has revealed.

His greatest fear is about to be realized in your decision to break every allegiance you ever had with his intentions.

Together we are forming an allegiance and partnership with God. We are ready to course correct, and leverage all that we have experienced and learned so that we can live, move, and have our being- yielded to his intentions.

Your Thoughts on "Perpetual Grace"

Listen and discern the instructions of the Spirit and obey. His grace is sufficient in the blind spots of life.

Every Season Is Your Season

See then that ye walk circumspectly, not as fools, but as wise, redeeming the time, because the days are evil. Wherefore be ye not unwise, but understanding what the will of the Lord is.
—Ephesians 5:15-17 KJV

The more you practice choosing God's way the easier it will become. We get to choose daily whether we will walk wisely and discern the season or not. It is not too late for us to live intentionally in step with purpose.

I am not telling you it will always be easy, but I am declaring it is necessary. When it feels impossible, ask for help: *"Lord, help me to want your way and yield the right of way to you in my life."*

If I were your enemy, I would do everything I could to convince you that it is too late. I can relate to this temptation and am certain that I am not alone. Oh, but the help of the Holy Spirit has been an escort for me and has provided an exit from this temptation, every time.

We can live in the assurance that it is not too late yet feel the pressure to redeem the time. I think we need the pressure to keep us aware of the urgency. The sense of urgency will motivate us to get back in step when we miss the mark. I have learned that an intimate relationship with the Lord is the only way to ensure that the pressure will produce obedience.

The absence of this pressure should set off all types of alarms in our spirit. I want to sense the pressure so deep in my spirit that it is more than a feeling but a knowing. I have learned that the power to live on purpose is not in what I feel but in what I know.

I have lived long enough to know a few things about my God. I know he is for me and has my best interest in mind. I know that I always have his attention. Yes, I know that my emotions will rarely agree with him, so I must govern them and not allow them to be the sole decision maker in my life. Yes, these things I know. I do not have to feel it to know it.

And ye shall know the truth, and the truth shall make you free.
—**John 8:32 KJV**

We learned the power of the word *knowing*. In Scripture, it literally means *intimacy*. In this verse, John is telling us to get in relationship with truth because the relationship will produce freedom. Jesus said that he is the way, the *truth,* and the life (John 14:6).

So we can confidently conclude that truth is a person, not information. My relationship with the Son will make me free (John 8:36). Freedom from what? Anything and everything—and that includes wrong thinking, wrong feeling, and wrong living.

You may be on a side road in the wilderness of life and thinking, *"That sounds good, Yolanda, but you do not know what I have done and where I have been."* What I do know is that this book was inspired by the Holy Spirit with you in mind. I am familiar with the side roads in the wilderness. I have traveled there a time or two myself. More importantly, God already had a plan to make our scenic route and every detail of our distractions and detours work for our good, if we will simply yield and surrender to him.

Catch this: God had a plan for reconciliation before we ever took our first wrong turn. I am living in a freedom that I have never known before. I have more questions than answers, but I am encouraged by *knowing,* I am living on purpose.

Redeeming the time because the days are evil.
—**Ephesians 5:16 KJV**

Paul is saying there is an opportunity to recover time that has been lost for varying reasons. I believe one of the ways God allows us to redeem time is by leveraging our experiences as currency in the lives of those who need to be ransomed from the bondage of the evil one. Sometimes an opportunity to minister from a place of experience will speed up reconciliation.

There is so much to be thankful for, despite our struggles. He releases strategies for reconciliation, reveals paths through resistance, provides an escort and an exit out of temptation, and gives us stamina for the hard places.

We have been given everything we need to fulfill his purpose. He orchestrates relationships of uncommon favor. He gives prophetic perspectives *(the ability to see God's way)*, resources, and know-how.

Yes, we have everything we need to live on purpose. On top of it all, he extends perpetual grace. We are well equipped.

Yielding is the key.

It takes longer to yield for some more than for others. However, because we do not have an eternity to fulfill our assignments in time, sooner is better than later. Tomorrow is not promised.

Two of the oldest lies of the enemy are (1) it is too late, and (2) there is no hurry. Don't fall for his lies. It is not too late to begin, but you must pick up the tempo because you don't have time to waste.

Can you sense the urgency in Paul's text in Ephesians? To me, it sounds like this: *Hurry up and carefully consider how you are walking! Be wise and recover lost time because the days are evil, and it will only get worse.*

It is the will of God that none should perish, so we need to get busy. We have kingdom work to do in the ripe fields of this world. Our revelation of who we are and why we are should provoke us to be productive harvesters.

Jesus gave us his assessment and told us that the harvest is plentiful, but the laborers are few (see Matthew 9:37; Luke 10:2). That was, and remains, a call to action—a call to partnership in purpose. We must gather the harvest while we still have time.

As we steward our revelation, I believe it will empower and illuminate our path forward, in his purpose.

By his divine power, God has given us everything we need for living a godly life. We have received all of this by coming to know him, the one who called us to himself by means of his marvelous glory and excellence. —**2 Peter 1:3 NLT**

A godly life is a purpose-filled life; so we have an assurance that if we do our part and remain diligent in this partnership, we cannot fail.

So, dear brothers and sisters, work hard to prove that you really are among those God has called and chosen. Do these things, and you will never fall away. —**2 Peter 1:10 NLT**

No, it is not too late for us. In these final few pages, allow me to encourage you that every season is your season.

I have heard it said, *"It's my season!"* or *"Your season is coming!"* or, here is a popular one: *"Your season of harvest is coming!"* The saying is often only in association with receiving something temporary rather than something eternal.

Can I be honest? It has annoyed my *whole soul* to the point that when I hear it, my spirit screams, *"Every season is my season!"*

I am not waiting for a good season to come my way; I am living on purpose in the season that I am in. Whether it is a season of wilderness or a season of promise. Whether it is a season of gathering or a season of planting. Whether it is a season of mourning or a season of joy, it is my season. Reconciliation is not seasonal. There is work to be done in *every* season.

Purpose is too complex, with its elements of multiplicity, to be confined to a season here or there. Allow me to remind you that God's purpose has been in motion before we were in our mother's wombs. Then, at a *Kairos* moment (*a point in time when conditions are right for the opportune and decisive moment*) he released us into time to begin walking it out.

We are speaking spirits and living souls released on this earth to partner with God's plans. Spiritual harvesting and discipleship are not seasonal work; they are *eternally significant kingdom work.*

Purpose is an everyday journey, not a seasonal experience. Therefore, every season is our season. It is not too late. You are not too young or too old or too lost or too rich or too poor. You have not sinned too much to be disqualified for his purpose right now.

All of us—flaws and all—were considered when God chose us in him before the foundation of the world.

So let us press and push back against the things in life that are meant to distract, discourage, and deter us from God's purpose. Share this book with anyone who will listen. They need it.

Purpose is calling. Simply respond with a resounding, *"Yes, Lord, I yield."* Then listen and allow him to customize the conversation. The world is waiting for more of the sons and daughters of God to live on purpose.

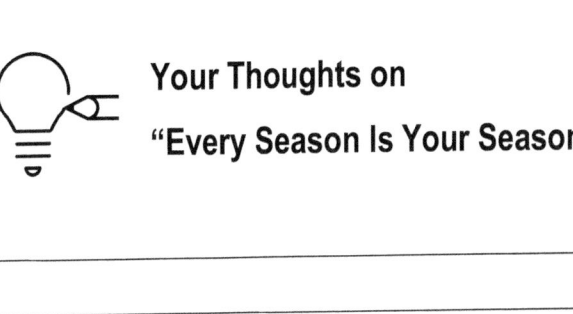

Your Thoughts on "Every Season Is Your Season"

The world is waiting for more of the sons and daughters of God to live on purpose.

About the Author

After serving twenty-nine years in the U.S. Army and retiring with the rank of Lieutenant Colonel, Yolanda G. Stewart is now executive pastor of Mosaic Church in Tennessee. Mosaic is a multi-campus, international ministry where for more than nine years Yolanda has served as a mentor to elders, pastors, and staff. In addition, she is a Bible teacher, recording artist, author, inventor, and entrepreneur.

Yolanda has been a conference speaker and leader for Christian and corporate audiences across the United States and beyond. She also serves as executive director for two non-profit organizations: Going Local Initiative (committed to providing affordable housing) and Wilma's Hope (committed to making accessibility modifications for senior adult homeowners).

Yolanda is a graduate of Wright State University, with a bachelor's degree in organizational communication. She is also the author of *Determined to Believe Again* (2009) and *The Little Books That Everyone Should Read* series.

Yolanda would tell you that, Isaiah 50:4 (NIV) best defines her mission in life: *"The Sovereign LORD has given me a well-instructed tongue, to know the word that sustains the weary. He wakens me morning by morning, wakens my ear to listen like one being instructed"*.

Yolanda enjoys traveling around the country to run half-marathons. She loves to hike, camp, and explore the beauty of God's creation with Damon, her high school sweetheart and husband of thirty-six years, along with their grandchildren. Yolanda and Damon reside in Clarksville, Tennessee, where they enjoy family dinners, bonfires, and conversations in the company of their three adult children and their families.

If you can beat it in your mind, you can beat it in your life -Ron Carpenter Jr.

You will change the trajectory of your life by changing your mind about the purpose for your life. Purpose is an amalgamation of God's intentions and his invitation to partner with him. By yielding to his intention, you are accepting his invitation to partnership opportunities. May yielding become our lifestyle.

Dear reader, my final words to you is this prayer:

Father, I pray that you will do unto them as you have done unto me. Reveal yourself through and beyond the conversation that began here in this book. Draw them into the place of grace and peace that comes with learning and understanding your will for their life. May they live and rest in the knowing and yielding.

In the great and mighty name of the Lord Jesus Christ -Amen.

www.ingramcontent.com/pod-product-compliance
Lightning Source LLC
Chambersburg PA
CBHW071120160426
43196CB00013B/2648